Iain R Spink is a fifth-generation fish smoker who, like his father before him, works tirelessly to elevate the humble Arbroath Smokie from a local speciality to nationwide delicacy. Regarded as an ambassador for the Arbroath Smokie, Iain's dedication, passion and enthusiasm for the product has led to many prestigious national awards, including being crowned 2006 BBC Food Producer of the Year. He has featured in numerous newspaper, magazine and book articles and made many TV appearances, giving him the opportunity to demonstrate the ancient process and relate its fascinating history to a much wider audience. Iain continues to promote Arbroath Smokies throughout the year at farmers' markets and various events around the country.

GW00640679

2006 BBC Rad
Winn

2006 UKT
Scottish Ch

2007 Waitr
Winner, Best Fresh Produce

2007 Daily Telegraph Taste of Britain –
Gold Award Winner, Best Regional Produce

2008 Waitrose Small Producer Awards –
Finalist, Best Food Producer

2009 Scottish Countryside Alliance
'Rural Hero' Awards – Finalist

2012 Great Taste Awards – 3★ Gold Winner

2012 Great Taste Awards – Top 50 Great British Foods

2012 Great Taste Awards –
Best Scottish Speciality Finalist

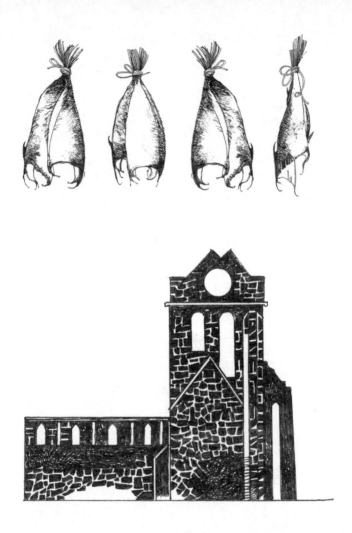

The
Arbroath Smokie
Bible

Iain R Spink

BIRLINN

First published in 2013 by
Birlinn Limited
West Newington House
10 Newington Road
Edinburgh
EH9 1QS

www.birlinn.co.uk

ISBN: 978 1 78027 733 2

British Library Cataloguing-in-Publication Data

A catalogue record for this book is available from
the British Library

Typeset by Mark Blackadder

Printed and bound by Bell & Bain Ltd, Glasgow

Contents

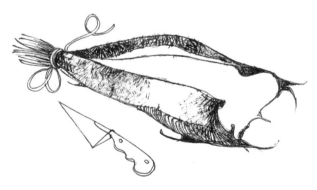

This book is dedicated to my father,

Robert Ritchie Spink,

for whose guidance I will always be grateful

Acknowledgements

Thanks to Nichola Fletcher for casting her experienced and knowledgeable eyes over my efforts and keeping me in the right direction. A special thanks to my wife Su for all her help and for her considerable time spent co-ordinating and cooking the recipes.

Thanks also to Angela Boggiano, Stephen Hill, Sue Lawrence, Nell Nelson and Jan Rees for their recipe contributions.

And last, but far from least, thanks to my very good friend Alex Spink for his continuing goodwill and generosity, without which my Arbroath Smokie-making days would be very different!

Iain R Spink
2013

To a Smokie

For haggis some wad live an' dee,
For Cullen skink or partan bree,
For Athole brose or kedgeree,
Or hokey-pokey;
Gie me that treasure o' the sea,
An Arbroath Smokie.
The end of ilka month's first week,
To Doubledykes just see me streak,
The Farmers' Market there to seek,
An' in twa blinks,
I'll hae a haddie at its peak,
Hot-smoked by Spink's.
First, heidless, gutless fish they wale,

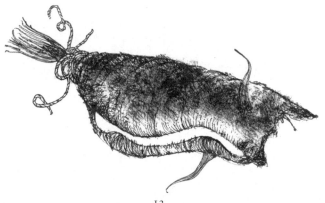

Tied up thegither by the tail,
An' hing them ower a wooden rail
That then they steek,
To cook them through, frae bane to scale,
In vats o' reek.
Then frae the smoke the fish are whipped,
An' each oot on the coonter's tipped,
Whaur frae the flesh the banes are ripped
By fingers nifty,
Till ane inside my poke is slipped,
For twa pund fifty.
Mony there are wha canna wait,
But pree theirs in the market straight;
I like to set mine on a plate,
Warm frae the grill;
Then royally I dine in state,
An' eat my fill.
O Smokie, when I see you there,
Your riggs o' ripened meat laid bare,
An' scent your fragrance on the air,
I bless them both:
The fisherfolk wha bring sic fare,
An' thee, Arbroath!

Dr Christopher MacLachlan
School of English
University of St Andrews
October 2009

Introduction

Arbroath Smokies are one of Scotland's best-known and best-loved traditional fish delicacies. They take their name from the small coastal town in the county of Angus, in the north-east of Scotland. Alongside their also famous fishy relatives, Finnan haddies and Loch Fyne kippers, they are perhaps the finest surviving example of the Scottish fishing industry's heritage. Arbroath Smokies and Finnan haddies are both made using haddock but kippers are made from herring. All three demonstrate methods of fish preservation, with both salt and smoke being used primarily to prolong their storage qualities and also to provide an alternative flavour experience. However, whereas the kippers and Finnans have been cold-smoked and require cooking before eating, the Arbroath Smokies have uniquely been hot-smoked – cooked and smoked at the same time – making them ready to eat straight from the smoker.

History

The Arbroath Smokie originates not from Arbroath as you might expect but from Auchmithie, a small fishing village approximately three miles up the coast from Arbroath. Although no one truly knows the origin of the Arbroath Smokie, I believe it began in the early part of the 11th century when the Viking settlers landed on our shores. There is some evidence to support this theory contained within George Hay's *History of Arbroath* (published 1895). Those early settlers brought with them many skills, including fish preservation, and I consider that it is from there that the Arbroath Smokie began its life. There are, to this day, very similar fish-smoking activities going on in Scandinavian countries further reinforcing this distant link. Another theory often touted about the Arbroath Smokie's origins relates back to a cottage in the village where some salted haddock were hanging up to dry as part of their preservation process. Unfortunately, a fire broke out and the entire house was

razed to the ground. It was then (reputedly) that, whilst sifting through the rubble, ashes, dust and other associated debris, the 'smokies' were discovered! I think it is more than a little unlikely that, having just seen their house destroyed, the occupants (or anyone else for that matter) would have picked up a blackened, dust-covered fish and then eaten it! This romanticised version of the Arbroath Smokie's true origin is still related around the harbour area in Arbroath known as 'the Fit o' the Toon' (the Foot of the Town) but the story probably holds as much water as the cremated fish in question.

However, we are still in Auchmithie so where does

Arbroath come into this? During the heyday of the late 19th century, fisher people began to move to Arbroath, lured by better housing, a better harbour and overall improved prospects promised by the town council of the time. They, with their skills and their labours, settled in the aforementioned 'Fit o' the Toon' and became one of the greatest contributors to Arbroath's economy. Their 'Arbroath' smokie inadvertently created something which was to become the signature of Arbroath and which, perhaps more than anything else, made Arbroath a household word throughout the country and even overseas. Sadly, however, Auchmithie's harbour is now in ruins and there have been no commercial landings of fish there for around 80 years. The 'Arbroath Smokie' is the only remaining legacy of Auchmithie's fishing community.

The production of Arbroath Smokies is still very much a small-scale cottage industry with only about a dozen producers left. At one time, however, there would have been many more (perhaps 50–60) little smokehouses dotted all over the 'Fit o' the Toon' with a 'barrel' smoking away out the back in a converted shed or similar type of shelter. Even then, production was relatively small as the Arbroath Smokie was only one of several fish products being produced. Having its own harbour and fish market meant that there was nearly always plenty of fish from which to choose, therefore the fish merchants would also process and sell various types of fillets (lemon sole, dabs, plaice, whiting, cod) as well as Finnans, shellfish etc. None would have relied on smokies as their sole source of income. When I was still working in the family business (RR Spink and Sons), we supplied several UK supermarkets with Arbroath Smokies for a number of years but the new owners of the company had other priorities and discontinued this sales avenue.

Although it is only haddock that is used to make Arbroath Smokies, the local fishermen of bygone days would have smoked many different types of fish, largely dictated by seasonal availability. Other white fish species such as whiting, codling and pollack would have been smoked in this way as well as flatfish such as dabs, soles and plaice. In the summer months, pelagic fish such as herring and mackerel would have provided a real seasonal treat. The very fact that haddock are available and abundant nearly all the year round is no doubt the main reason why they are the 'chosen ones' with which to make Arbroath Smokies, though I am quite sure that it is also down to their uniquely beautiful delicate flavour. In my opinion, North Sea haddock have a far superior flavour to those caught in most other waters.

In the past, as well as the regular household duties, it was the women who did all the preparation and smoking of the fish while the men and boys were at sea in all weathers trying to catch them. Those same hardy women would also carry their men folk over the beach on their backs and deposit them into the boat so that their feet would be kept dry whilst out at sea.

The Process

The process used to make an Arbroath Smokie has changed little over the centuries despite all of the modern technology and techniques that are now available and widely used in food processing and manufacture. Nowadays many smoke-houses use big stainless steel kilns which are almost entirely controlled by computer programmes. Whilst these shiny steel boxes may yield satisfactory results for many types of fish, meats, cheeses etc, the unique conditions required to create a perfect Arbroath Smokie cannot be replicated so easily. Arbroath Smokies are still made by very old and traditional methods – the rustic brick 'kilns' used today in Arbroath are adapted only slightly from the original wooden 'smoking barrels' that I still uniquely use and that were also used by my ancestors. I think there is a sheer honesty in the process of a lightly salted fresh fish being smoked and cooked over a log fire inside a halved barrel, emerging ready to eat. It has a great deal of appeal not only to connoisseurs of fine food but to us all, as it takes us back to an age where everything was so much simpler and free from interference.

The Arbroath Smokie-making process is quite a lengthy one and begins with the buying of the fish at auction on the fish market. In the past, all the fish that were used to make smokies were caught and landed locally by small inshore fishing boats. However, with the general decline in the fishing industry over the last couple of decades, almost all of the north-east fishing ports have gone, meaning I now have to go much further afield to source my haddock – usually Peterhead, 100 miles away. The quality of raw material is absolutely paramount here as I will only use the freshest available haddock to make my Arbroath Smokies – the old proverb that you can't make a silk purse out of a sow's ear springs to mind. No amount of smoking and salting will ever make a good Arbroath Smokie out of a poor quality haddock.

Obtaining the perfect fish to make Arbroath Smokies is not as easy as you might think as there are many factors and variables to consider. Like most things in life, there is good and not so good and this can apply to fishing boats as well. Many fish buyers

have their own favourite boats that they like to buy from whenever possible at the fish auction – as well as those that they tend to avoid. A buyer is looking for fish that are of the correct size, that are as fresh as possible, possess a firm flesh, are preferably hand gutted and have all their scales intact. And, very importantly, I look for boxes with good weights of fish in them – some less scrupulous boats deliberately put excess amounts of ice in the bottom of the boxes to deceive careless buyers!

Once bought, the fish are transported back to the fish house where the heads are then removed and the belly cavity is cleaned out. The next stage is salting. This important and essential part of the process draws out excess water from the fish and toughens up the skin in readiness for smoking. A dry salting process is used rather than a brine solution. Experience plays a particularly important role here as the length of time that the fish lie in the salt has to be adjusted to suit the particular requirements of each batch of fish. Generally, large and/or very fresh fish need a longer time in the salt than smaller or slightly older fish. This must be done correctly. Not enough salt and they won't smoke properly and their potential storage time will be reduced. Conversely, too much salt and the smokies' beautiful delicate flavour will be compromised. During their time in the salt, the fish are matched up into equal-sized pairs and tied by the tails using a short jute string. Jute, a versatile natural fibre, was produced locally from mills in Arbroath. It is an ideal material being not only very strong and durable but also inexpensive. After lying for the allocated time (anything from 1 to 24 hours), the tied fish are rinsed in clean fresh water to remove any excess remaining salt. They are then carefully hung on to special sticks or rails and left to drip for a short time.

Meanwhile the smoking kiln or 'barrel' is prepared. Arbroath Smokies are still smoked using the same old and

traditional methods from yesteryear; the only significant difference now is in the size of the kilns. Originally the 'kiln' was a small halved barrel partially sunk into the ground but this has now been replaced by larger brick-built constructions (approximately 2m by 1.25m). These bigger brick kilns are now used by all the smokie producers in Arbroath today with the exception of myself as I still uniquely smoke my fish in small batches using the same small halved wooden barrels that my ancestors used. The more uniform square shape and bigger physical size simply allow more fish to be done in each batch without unduly compromising the end result. A fire is built inside the barrel (even those using the brick kilns still refer to it as their 'barrel') using hardwood logs. This is typically any combination of ash, beech, birch, elm, oak or sycamore but virtually any hardwood can be used. Different woods unsurprisingly give different flavours of smoke but I like to use oak and beech whenever possible to ensure a degree of

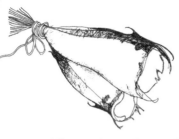

consistency in the taste associated with my own particular Arbroath Smokies. In past times, the wood used would have been driftwood gathered from the foreshore and also any fallen timber collected from nearby woodland. This random mixture of wood types must have made for some interesting flavours in the early smokies!

The sticks of paired fish are then placed over the barrel followed by a layer or two of dampened hessian sacking. These hessian bags or 'cloots' allow the fire to breathe and maintain the required heat. The number of layers and the level of dampening of the hessian depend largely on the weather conditions and may be adjusted throughout the smoking period to prevent the fish either smoking too quickly and burning or smoking too slowly and drying out. The water and juices dripping from the slowly smoking fish land on the hot embers below and make lots of steam, thus ensuring a very humid smoky atmosphere within the barrel, ultimately resulting in fish that are moist inside and a lovely golden brown colour on the outside. The

smoking time can vary considerably but is typically 40 minutes in my small barrel or up to perhaps 90 minutes in the slightly bigger kilns. No two batches take the same time to cook so a keen eye has to be kept on the fish as they are being smoked – no fancy digital timers here, just good old experience! An experienced smoker can judge exactly when the fish will be ready simply by looking at the colour of the fish skin as it changes whilst smoking from a shiny silver grey to a beautiful light golden brown. Of course, nowadays, records have to be kept so a temperature recording of the fish will be taken and duly noted.

The Arbroath Smokies produced today are very much an evolution of the Auchmithie originals. In those bygone days, there was no proper refrigeration available, making it difficult to keep produce from spoiling, so the fish were preserved by smoking, salting, pickling or drying, or even a combination of those methods. From pictorial evidence provided by The Fraser Collection circa 1900 (available to view at www.arbroathsmokies.com), it can be seen that the early smokies were indeed very different to their modern counterparts. Close inspection of the photographs reveals very dark

SMOKIES

smokies that have obviously been smoked very heavily and almost certainly been very heavily salted beforehand to enable them to be kept for a longer period of time without modern refrigeration. They may even have been required to be rehydrated in fresh water before eating. In contrast, today's Arbroath Smokies have been only lightly smoked and salted and, as a result, are very moist and juicy when first made and are intended to be stored and eaten within a relatively short timescale. Although they will keep for up to 10 days in the fridge, as with most fresh foods, smokies are undoubtedly best eaten as soon as they are made. A freshly made Arbroath Smokie plucked straight from the fire is truly one of the world's great tastes and should be on every foodie's tick list of things to try before you die.

My Background

Coming from a family with a history in the fish industry stretching back at least five generations, I suppose it was always inevitable that I would follow in the footsteps of my ancestors; it is probably true to say that it's in my blood. I first entered the family business RR Spink and Sons at the age of 15, with a part-time job after school as a delivery boy in our fish shop. I well remember teetering up to the train station on an old, heavy, black message bike, a huge basket on the front, loaded to the gunwales with parcels of smokies ready for despatch to destinations all over the country. At 17, I left school and began working full-time in the main fish house, learning every aspect of the fish trade from buying on the market through to

processing, storage and freezing. Making Arbroath Smokies was just one of the many skills I learnt during those years, however, it has proved to be the most valuable one.

My father Robert (Bob) was understandably a big influence on me and always set the highest standards possible. He recognised the potential for the Arbroath Smokie many years ago, tirelessly championing its virtues at every opportunity, building up the Spink brand to such a level that it has become virtually synonymous with Arbroath Smokies. His Arbroath Smokie promotion perhaps reached its peak in 2004 when, after three years spear-heading the campaign, his efforts were finally rewarded in the European Commission with the granting of a protected status – Protected Geographical Indication (PGI) – for the Arbroath Smokie; for more details see page 32. Those very high standards set by my father undoubtedly left their mark and have provided me with a very high benchmark to follow.

The family business changed ownership in 2001 and the new owners took the company in a different direction. This change, combined with my father's retirement shortly afterwards, led to me re-evaluating my own career. I decided on a fresh start and left the company to attend university and do an environmental science degree. It was during my time at university that I started up my own specialist smokie-making business which fortunately coincided with a real upsurge in interest in local, regional and traditionally produced foods. I knew, with the Arbroath Smokie, I had a truly world-class product but how could I get it out there and noticed by a much wider audience? My answer was to take the Arbroath Smokie right back to its ancient roots and exactly replicate the original smoking process, using wooden casks, hardwood logs and hessian bags, and then take it on the road, creating, in effect, an Arbroath Smokie roadshow. This cooking and smoking on site at various events and locations provides a valuable educational purpose by allowing customers not only to see the whole process before them but, most importantly, enabling them to enjoy a freshly made smokie at its best, straight from the fire. The allure provided by the rows of fish hanging up waiting to be smoked, coupled with the aromas generated from the burning hardwood log fire and the emergent golden brown smokies has proved to be a very popular attraction. My packed calendar sees me working every weekend of the year promoting smokies to a broad range of audiences, attending events such as the BBC Good Food Show, the Golf Open, T in the Park, the Royal Highland Show, Scone Game Fair, Dundee Food and Flower Show and many Highland Games, as well as a regular weekly slot at several Fife Farmers' Markets.

So how do you know
it's the real thing?

The Arbroath Smokie is now officially recognised at the highest levels in Europe as it has protection through the designation of a Protected Geographical Indication (PGI). PGI status is granted to products which are produced, processed or prepared within a definite geographical area and have clear associations with that area. This same status is also displayed on products such as champagne and Parma ham. This effectively means that the name 'Arbroath Smokie' can only be applied to haddock that have been smoked within an 8-km (5-mile) radius of Arbroath in accordance with the strict set of guidelines laid down in the PGI specification. So now, wherever you see Arbroath Smokies for sale, by law, the distinctive blue and yellow PGI logo should be prominently displayed beside them.

The push for protection was inspired by my father Bob Spink who almost single-handedly led the campaign through a two-year process on behalf of the fish processors of Arbroath. This involved defining the methods of production and, most importantly, defining the extent of the area within which Arbroath Smokies must be produced, making

sure of course to include the neighbouring village of Auchmithie from where Arbroath Smokies originated.

The recognition from Europe has ensured that the quality, tradition and identity of the Arbroath Smokie will be preserved, thus confirming its place as the signature product of Arbroath and one of the prides of Angus.

Alcoholic Accompaniments

It is always good to accompany a fine meal with a nice glass (or two) of wine. I am certainly no wine expert but I thought I would share a few of the ones that I like. Generally a lightly oaked white wine will go with smoked fish although, because there are almost as many types of smoked fish as there are white wines, finding the perfect match is not that easy. It also depends to an extent on what dish you have chosen to cook your smokie in as some of the heavier sauces require a wine that can cut through the creaminess of the dish.

Smoked fish and oaked wines share some characteristics in their make-up which marry together nicely when they are paired at the table. The wine will have been stored in a specially charred oak cask to allow it to develop flavours form the burnt wood, and the haddock has been slowly smoked over an oak wood fire; sometimes old barrels from the cooperage are burned so it is even remotely possible (though very unlikely) that the same barrel flavoured both products in its life!

There are several wines that would fit the bill to go with

your Arbroath Smokie dish. The Australian, Californian and South African Chardonnays are very oaky and may be a bit too overpowering for some palates whereas a classic-style, lightly oaked Chardonnay may have a broader appeal and be a perfect accompaniment to many of the dishes mentioned. Others such as Muscadet, Pinot Grigio and Semillon would all go perfectly well. However, for something completely different, try the Autumn Oak Leaf or Gooseberry fruit wine produced by the Cairn o' Mohr winery near Dundee.

Some of you might like a bottle of nice beer to go with your smokie and fortunately there are now a number of Scottish brewers producing some really superb ales. My favourites are the Yellowhammer from the Black Isle brewery and Avalanche from Fyne Ales. Another more local beer which I have been enjoying lately is the Crail Ale brewed by the St Andrews Brewing Company. Although

obviously different, each of them possesses a delicate citrus taste or aroma which seems to go well with smokies.

Arbroath Smokies are becoming increasingly popular on Burns Supper menus as a first course before the haggis and this has led to a number of my customers providing me with recommendations of whisky pairings to go with the smoked fish. Much as I enjoy a wee dram from time to time, I usually prefer it to be separate from my food, though I do enjoy sitting down occasionally with a plate of rough oatcakes, some Arbroath Smokie pâté and wee nip of a nice smoky malt like an Ardbeg. A couple of years ago, I was involved in a promotional exercise with Ardbeg where my Arbroath Smokies were paired up very nicely with their 10-year-old single malt and served together at several of their events. Like the aforementioned wine, whisky selection is a matter of personal taste and you will, no doubt, through time find your own particular favourites to go with your smokies.

Basics

The first thing that you have to do with an Arbroath Smokie is to remove the main bone that runs through the fish. This is VERY easy to do as long as you follow the guidelines!

Boning Instructions

For an instructional video tutorial of this process visit my website, www.arbroathsmokies.com or my facebook page 'IainRSpinkArbroathSmokies'.

Boning smokies straight from the refrigerator can be made much easier by first removing the fish from any packaging then warming gently in a microwave on medium power for around 30 seconds (1000W microwave). Twist off the tails to separate the two fish, then take one of the smokies and hold it belly side up, with the thick end towards you in one hand. Use your other hand to gently squeeze the fish from top to bottom along the middle of the smokie. Whilst doing this you should feel the flesh separating from the bone. Next break the skin from the belly cavity to the

tail and then gently open the fish up and pull out the whole intact bone. Once this main bone is out the smokie can be opened out and laid flat ready to be picked down and flaked into your dish or just used as it is. Most of the white meat has no bones in it now with only a few left down the sides where the lugs are. Once flaked down, depending on how particular or patient you are, the smokie should yield about 55–60% of its original weight. So, for a typical pair of smokies weighing 500g, you should get around 300g of flaked meat.

Storage Instructions

Being cooked, salted and smoked, Arbroath Smokies have

a good shelf life compared to fresh fish. From the day of smoking, they can be kept perfectly fresh for 10 days in the refrigerator or 17 days in a vacuum pack. They can still be safely kept for a little longer (two–three days) but the extra time in storage compromises the quality of the finished product. Vacuum-packed smokies will take on different flavours and textures the longer they are kept in the bag as the smoke permeates from the outer skin through into the delicate white flesh giving them an overly smoky flavour. Smokies bought 'loose' (not vac-packed) and kept in the fridge dry out a little through time so they should be kept covered whilst in storage. They can also be frozen and kept for up to three months though they will change considerably in both texture and flavour.

Tips for Cooking with Arbroath Smokies

1. You rarely need salt – the Arbroath Smokies have already been salted.
2. When a recipe requires butter, use unsalted butter.
3. If using stock cubes, try to use reduced salt ones.
4. When using Swiss cheeses, Emmental and Gruyère are often interchangeable in recipes but some Gruyère cheeses contain almost twice as much salt as Emmental so bear this in mind when making your dishes.
5. Similarly, many Grana Padano cheeses have less salt than Parmigiano-Reggiano ones.

Recipes – plain and simple

You do not have to cook an elaborate recipe to enjoy an Arbroath Smokie – a simple reheat with a bit of butter is as good a method as any. There are three main ways to do this:

Grill – this is probably the most popular way to heat smokies. Simply remove the bone, brush the white flesh with a little melted butter and gently reheat under a preheated grill for 3–4 minutes.

Microwave – remove the backbone, brush with butter but this time close the fish up, place in a covered dish and heat on medium power for 1 minute 30 seconds (1000W oven).

Conventional Oven – preheat the oven to 180°C/350°F/ Gas 4, remove the backbone, open out and generously dot with butter, close the fish up, place in a foil packet and heat in the oven for 15 minutes.

Like myself, one of Jamie Oliver's favourite ways to eat smokies is to simply reheat them under the grill with the addition of a little butter. I just dot some plain unsalted butter on my smokies but Jamie serves his with a generous knob of herb butter, grated nutmeg and lemon zest. Many herbs, such as coriander, parsley, chives, dill or lemon thyme, can be used either individually or in combinations according to personal preference.

I met Jamie when he invited me to make smokies for his *Jamie's Great Britain* series. The only snag was I had to go over to the west coast (Arbroath is on the east coast) where the entire Scottish part of the programme was being filmed. The location was stunning – right down on the beach of a sea loch surrounded by an incredible mountain backdrop. The film crew wanted me in the most scenic spot, of course, so I had the smokie barrel dug into the beach only a couple of metres from the estimated high-tide line! I had the fish smoking away nicely on the barrel and Jamie duly arrived by boat from his scallop-diving exploits round the coast a little. To say he enjoyed his freshly made smokie would be an understatement!

Soups and Starters

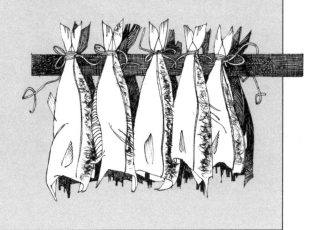

PARSLEY

LEEKS

Arbroath Smokie and Leek Chowder

This delicious soup is easy to make and provides a hearty, warming dish for a cold winter's day.

Serves: 4
Preparation Time: 10 minutes
Cooking Time: 30 minutes

Ingredients
1 tbsp olive oil
150g streaky bacon, diced
3 medium leeks, washed and sliced
2 bay leaves
2 medium potatoes, peeled and diced into small cubes
500ml fish or vegetable stock
500ml whole milk
1 pair Arbroath Smokies, boned and flaked
198g can sweetcorn, drained
142ml carton single cream
freshly ground black pepper
2 tbsp fresh parsley, roughly chopped

Heat the oil in a large saucepan and gently fry the bacon until starting to brown. Remove and reserve. Add the leeks, bay leaves and potatoes, and cook for a couple of minutes. Pour in the stock, bring to the simmer and cook for 10 minutes.

Remove the bay leaves from the pan. With a handheld blender, roughly process – do not make it a

puree. Add the reserved bacon and milk and simmer for
5 minutes.

Add the flaked Arbroath Smokies, sweetcorn and
cream to the saucepan. Season with black pepper and stir
in the parsley. Heat through gently and serve.

Cullen Spink

This variation of a very famous traditional Scottish soup was created by my father, Bob Spink. I once cooked this recipe on Auchmithie beach whilst filming for the *Andy Bates Street Feasts* TV series. I did the whole thing from scratch – smoking the fish first and then cooking the recipe on my camping stove! The main difference here is the inclusion of flaked Arbroath Smokies rather than the usual cold-smoked haddock fillet. Although very similar, I think the use of Arbroath Smokies in this recipe gives the soup a more delicate smoky flavour and a nicer texture than you get with the cold-smoked alternative. This soup is healthy, filling and easy to make – and, when served with some buttered granary bread, it is almost a meal in itself.

Serves: 4
Preparation Time: 15 minutes
Cooking Time: 45 minutes

Ingredients
1 pair Arbroath Smokies, boned and flaked
300ml water
2 onions, finely chopped
750g potatoes, peeled and thinly sliced
¼ tsp turmeric
pinch of cayenne pepper
475ml whole milk

25g unsalted butter
75ml double cream
2 tbsp fresh parsley, chopped

Place the flaked Arbroath Smokies in a medium saucepan with the water. Bring gently to the boil and immediately set aside from the heat. Do not break the flakes further. After 10 minutes, using a slotted spoon, lift the fish from the water and set aside on a plate.

Strain the cooking liquid into a bowl. Clean the saucepan and return the cooking liquid to it. Add the onions, potatoes, turmeric and cayenne. Cover the pan and cook until the potatoes are soft, about 20–25 minutes.

When the potatoes are cooked, remove the pan from the heat. Mash the potatoes with the onions and the cooking liquid using a potato masher. Gradually add the milk, stirring constantly, until it is blended with the potatoes. Return the pan to a low heat.

Add the flaked Arbroath Smokies and butter. Cook the mixture until it is hot, gently stirring, but do not boil. Taste and add salt if necessary (remember the Arbroath Smokies already contain salt).

Serve in bowls, adding a swirl of cream to the centre and garnishing with a little chopped fresh parsley.

Arbroath Smokies and Parsnip Soup

There are some chefs whose style of cooking particularly appeals to me and Sue Lawrence is certainly one of them. A previous winner of BBC's *Masterchef* and author of many fine cookery books, Sue's passion for traditional Scottish recipes and her emphasis on using local produce hit the right notes with me. Sue first visited me at Cupar Farmers' Market some years ago and used my smokies to create this lovely tasty soup.

Serves: 4
Preparation Time: 15 minutes
Cooking Time: 45 minutes

Ingredients
2 tbsp extra virgin olive oil, plus a little extra for drizzling
1 onion, peeled and chopped
2 garlic cloves, peeled and chopped
2 celery sticks, peeled and chopped
2 tsp ground cumin
1kg parsnips, peeled and chopped
1.2 litres hot chicken stock
salt and pepper
50ml dry white wine
1 pair Arbroath Smokies

Heat 2 tbsp oil in a saucepan and gently fry the onion, garlic and celery for about 10 minutes. Add the cumin and stir. Add the parsnips and stir to coat in the oil. Cook for about 5 minutes then add the hot stock and a little salt and pepper and bring to the boil. Cover, reduce to a simmer and cook for about 25 minutes or until tender.

Tip into a liquidiser or blender with the wine, puree until smooth and then check the seasoning. Meanwhile, wrap the smokies in foil and heat in a low oven for 10–15 minutes. Bone and flake the warm smokies. To serve, ladle the soup into warm bowls, top with smokies and drizzle with oil.

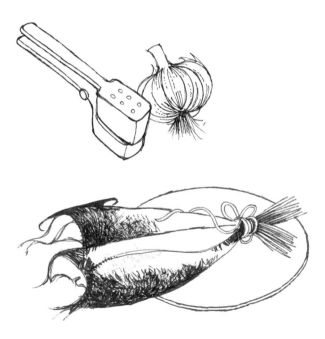

Smokie Pots

The following recipe is kindly reproduced with Sue Lawrence's permission and can be found in her book *A Cook's Tour of Scotland*. You can add a free-range egg per pot if you like. Break one into each pot on top of the spinach, season and then spoon the sauce over. Bake as instructed below until the yolk is almost set.

Serves: 4
Preparation Time: 10 minutes
Cooking Time: 20 minutes

Ingredients
200g spinach, cooked until wilted and patted thoroughly
25g butter
25g plain flour
300ml whole milk
1 pair Arbroath Smokies, boned and flaked
40g freshly grated Grana Padano cheese
salt and freshly ground black pepper

Preheat the oven to 190°C/375°F/Gas 5.

Place the spinach in the base of each of four ramekins. Season lightly.

Melt the butter in a pan, add the flour and stir well. Cook for 1 minute, stirring, then add the milk gradually and cook for 3–4 minutes or until thickened. Season to taste and add the flaked Arbroath Smokies.

Spoon the sauce over the spinach and then top with the cheese. Bake for 12–15 minutes or until golden and bubbling. (If you are adding the eggs, cook for no more than 14 minutes).

Serve with plenty of good bread.

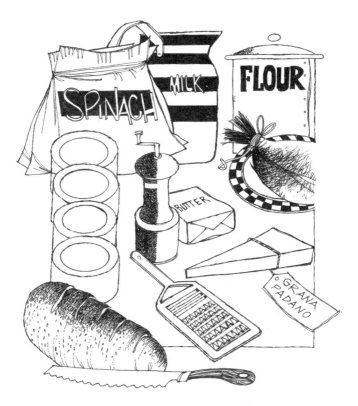

Luxury Smoked Fish Terrine

This makes a very elegant starter, particularly for a dinner party. It MUST be very well chilled before serving. I only use (and sell!) Loch Duart smoked salmon. I believe that their exemplary environmental credentials and fish husbandry result in farmed salmon of the finest quality available, bar none. For more details, go to www.lochduart.com.

Serves: 10–12
Preparation Time: 30 minutes
Chilling Time: Overnight

Ingredients
2 x 200g Loch Duart cold-smoked salmon
1 pair hot-smoked trout, boned and flaked
500g full-fat soft cheese
3 level tbsp horseradish sauce
3 tbsp lemon juice
½ tsp cayenne pepper
250ml double cream
1 pair Arbroath Smokies, boned and flaked
freshly ground black pepper
sprigs of dill for decoration
wedges of lemon, to serve

Line a small loaf tin with cling film, leaving enough extra to cover the whole tin at the end of preparation. Carefully line the tin with the sliced salmon, reserving enough to cover the top and set aside.

Place the flaked smoked trout in a bowl with 300g of cream cheese, the horseradish sauce, 2 tbsp lemon juice, ½ tsp cayenne. Mix using a hand-held blender. Add the double cream a little at a time, blending in at each stage until you reach a moist but still firm consistency, taking care not to let the mixture get too thin. This could be as much as 150ml but you may find you require less.

Place the flaked Arbroath Smokies in a bowl with 200g of cream cheese and 1 tbsp lemon juice and season with black pepper. Mix using a hand-held blender. Add the double cream a little at a time, blending in at each stage until you reach a moist but still firm consistency, taking care not to let the mixture get too thin. This could be as much as 100ml, but you may find you require less.

Layer the fish mixtures into the tin, putting half of the smoked trout mixture in first, then all of the Arbroath Smokie mixture and finish with the remaining half of the smoked trout. Cover the top with any remaining cold-smoked salmon. Draw the excess cling film over the top of the tin and place in a refrigerator overnight.

Once properly chilled turn out of the tin and decorate with small sprigs of dill. To serve, slice with a sharp knife and accompany each with a wedge of lemon.

This would go well with a small salad of fresh leaves and cherry tomatoes.

Arbroath Smokie Pâté

I make this lovely pâté every week for my regular farmers' market customers and it flies off the table. A nice alternative is to use a pair of hot-smoked trout, adding 2 tbsp horseradish sauce to the recipe below and replacing the black pepper with a pinch of cayenne pepper.

Serves: 10
Preparation Time: 15 minutes
Chilling Time: 1 hour

Ingredients
1 pair Arbroath Smokies, boned and flaked
250g full-fat cream cheese
juice of half a lemon
150ml double cream
black pepper

Put the flaked Arbroath Smokies, cream cheese and lemon juice in a bowl. Process with a hand-held blender until well combined. Gradually add double cream, blending between each addition, until you reach your desired consistency – you may not need the full amount of cream. Spoon into a serving dish or ramekins and sprinkle with black pepper to decorate.

Chill for at least 1 hour.

Serve with good quality oatcakes.

Main Courses

PGI Pie

Well, it is a quiche actually but that did not rhyme with PGI! What is PGI? See page 32! I have taken the opportunity to combine two PGI products to make a tasty savoury dish. This is just as good eaten hot or cold. Still on the PGI theme, you could even enjoy a glass of champagne with it!

Serves: 6
Preparation Time: 40 minutes
Cooking Time: 40 minutes

Ingredients
250g ready-made shortcrust pastry
1 pair Arbroath Smokies, boned and flaked
2 tbsp thyme, chopped
80g Parma ham
150ml whole milk
150ml single cream
finely grated zest of 1 lemon
3 medium free-range eggs
freshly ground black pepper
40g Scottish mature Cheddar, grated

Preheat the oven to 200°C/400°F/Gas 6.

Roll out the pastry on a lightly floured surface and use it to line a 23cm loose-base tart tin with a 4cm depth; trim excess. Line with greaseproof paper, fill with baking beans and bake blind for 15 minutes. Remove paper and beans, and bake for a further 5 minutes.

Reduce the oven temperature to 180°C/350°F/Gas 4.

Scatter the flaked Arbroath Smokies into the case and sprinkle with thyme. Scatter three-quarters of the Parma ham into the case – it will shred naturally as you pull the slices away from the interleafing paper.

Beat together the milk, cream, lemon zest, eggs and black pepper and pour into the case. Scatter with the cheese and then the remaining Parma ham.

Bake for around 40 minutes until golden and set.

Arbroath Smokie Mediterranean Puff

Serves: 2–3
Preparation Time: 10 minutes
Cooking Time: 30 minutes

Ingredients
2 tbsp olive oil
2 medium red onions, sliced
250g ready-made puff pastry
150ml full-fat crème fraîche
1 pair Arbroath Smokies, boned and flaked
75g sun-dried tomatoes, drained and chopped
50g pitted green olives, sliced
freshly ground black pepper
1 free-range egg yolk, lightly beaten
handful of basil leaves.

Preheat the oven to 200°C/400°F/Gas Mark 6.

Heat the oil in a heavy-based pan and cook the onion gently over a low heat for 5–8 minutes until soft.

Meanwhile, roll the pastry out to a rectangle, approximately 22cm x 32cm. Place on a baking tray and prick with a fork leaving a 2cm border.

Spread the crème fraîche over the pastry but not the border. Top with the red onion, flaked Arbroath Smokies, sun-dried tomatoes and green olives.

Season with freshly ground black pepper and a

drizzle of olive oil. Glaze the border with the egg yolk.

Place in the oven and cook for 15–20 minutes or until golden brown.

Scatter over the basil leaves and serve with a crisp green salad.

Arbroath Smokie and Cheese Tart

Serves: 4
Preparation Time: 35 minutes
Cooking Time: 35 minutes

Ingredients
250g ready-made shortcrust pastry
2 large free-range eggs
150ml whole milk
1 tbsp Dijon mustard
100g half-fat crème fraîche
50ml double cream
freshly ground black pepper
1 pair Arbroath Smokies, boned and flaked
150g Emmental cheese, grated
2 tbsp fresh chives, chopped

Preheat the oven to 200°C/400°F/Gas 6.

Roll out the pastry on a lightly floured surface and use to line a 23cm loose-base tart tin with a 4cm depth; trim excess. Line with greaseproof paper, fill with baking beans and bake blind for 15 minutes. Remove paper and beans, and bake for a further 5 minutes.

Reduce the oven temperature to 180°C/350°F/Gas Mark 4.

Whisk together the eggs, milk, mustard, crème fraîche, cream and season with black pepper.

Scatter the flaked Arbroath Smokies into the pastry case. Cover with 100g of the Emmental and most of the

chives. Pour over the egg and milk mixture, and then top
with the remaining cheese and the rest of the chives.

Bake for 35 minutes or until firm and golden brown.

Arbroath Smokie Tartlets

This recipe is based on Nell Nelson's Smoked Haddock
Tartlets. I met Nell in 2006 when filming for the TV
series *The Woman Who Ate Scotland*. In her original recipe,
Nell makes her own pastry but I have used ready-made
for ease and speed! This can be served as tartlets or,
alternatively, as a single large quiche.

Serves: 6
Preparation Time: 30 minutes
Cooking Time: 50 minutes

Ingredients
250g shortcrust pastry
1 leek, white part only, finely chopped
knob of unsalted butter
2 tbsp double cream
1 pair Arbroath Smokies, boned and flaked
1 tomato, sliced
1 free-range egg, lightly beaten
2 tbsp breadcrumbs
1 tbsp chopped dill
pinch cayenne pepper

pinch ground nutmeg
pinch ground black pepper
1 small wedge of lemon
100g Scottish mature Cheddar cheese, grated

Preheat the oven to 200°C/400°F/Gas 6.

Roll out the pastry on a lightly floured surface and use to line 6 tartlet cases; trim excess. Line the tartlet cases with greaseproof paper circles. Fill them with baking beans and bake blind for 10–15 minutes. Remove the paper and bake for another 5 minutes until the pastry is light golden.

Reduce the oven temperature to 180°C/350°F/Gas 4.

Meanwhile gently fry the leeks in the butter over a low heat until soft, but not coloured – about 5 minutes. Stir in the cream and flaked Arbroath Smokies, cook for a minute. Add the tomato and remove from the heat.

Stir the egg, breadcrumbs, dill, cayenne, nutmeg and pepper into the mixture and squeeze over the lemon juice. Pile the mixture into the prepared tart cases, sprinkle liberally with the cheese and bake for 20 minutes or until tops are golden.

Serve with a fresh salad.

Luxury Fish Pie

This is a fantastic fish pie and a family favourite. If you wish, as an option, you can top with grated cheese.

Serves: 6
Preparation Time: 35 minutes
Cooking Time: 20 minutes

Ingredients
1kg floury potatoes (Rooster or Maris Piper), peeled and halved if large
100g unsalted butter
600ml whole milk
200g white fish fillet, such as cod, haddock, whiting or coley, skinned
200g fresh salmon fillet, skinned
1 onion, thickly sliced
4 cloves
2 bay leaves
1 pair Arbroath Smokies, boned and flaked
100g peeled prawns
50g plain flour
salt and freshly ground black pepper
pinch freshly grated nutmeg
small bunch parsley, chopped

Preheat oven to 200°C/400°F/Gas 6.

Boil the potatoes for 20 minutes. Drain, season and mash with half of the butter and a splash of the milk.

Meanwhile, put the white fish and salmon in a large

saucepan or frying pan and pour over the remainder of the milk. Add the onion, cloves and bay leaves. Bring the milk gently to the boil, reduce the heat and simmer for 8 minutes. Lift the fish out, flake into large pieces into a large baking dish and then add the flaked Arbroath Smokies and prawns. Strain the milk and reserve.

Melt the remaining half of the butter in a pan, stir in the flour and cook for 1 minute over moderate heat, taking care not to burn. Take off the heat, pour in a little of the reserved milk, then stir until blended. Continue to add the milk gradually, mixing well until you have a smooth sauce. Return to the heat, bring to the boil and cook for 5 minutes, stirring continually until it has thickened a little. Season with salt, pepper and nutmeg, and then pour over the fish.

Top the pie with the mashed potatoes, making sure that it goes right to the edges of the dish. Bake for 20 minutes. Serve garnished with chopped parsley.

Arbroath Smokie and Pea Risotto

This recipe uses cream cheese to obtain a creamy finish but, if you prefer your risotto to be more traditional, omit the cream cheese and, at the end of cooking the rice, beat in 50g of unsalted butter, followed by 100g Grana Padano cheese, before adding the fish and peas.

Serves: 4
Preparation Time: 10 minutes
Cooking Time: 25 minutes

Ingredients
1 tbsp olive oil
25g unsalted butter
small bunch of spring onions – white parts finely sliced,
    green parts chopped
1 bay leaf
2 tbsp fresh thyme
400g Arborio rice
1 glass white wine
700ml fish or vegetable stock
150g peas, frozen
100g full-fat cream cheese
2 pairs Arbroath Smokies, boned and flaked

Melt the olive oil and butter in a large saucepan and cook the spring onions for 2–3 minutes. Add the bay leaf, thyme and rice and cook for a further 2 minutes.

Pour in the white wine and stir until it has been

absorbed. Add the stock a little at a time and stir occasionally until absorbed. This will take about 15–20 minutes. There should still be a little bite in the rice. Remove the bay leaf.

Meanwhile, cook the peas in boiling water for 4 minutes. Drain and reserve.

Add the cream cheese and stir until melted through the rice. Add the flaked Arbroath Smokies and peas and heat through gently.

Serve in large bowls.

Nichola Fletcher's Arbroath Smokie Recipes

Nichola is well known not only for her Fletcher's venison brand but also as a cook and food writer. She has written numerous food books and has a real passion for traditional and locally produced foods. I first met Nichola through trading at the Fife Farmers' Markets. Her venison was responsible for turning me from a pesco-vegetarian back into a meat eater again! Remarkably, the two of us were both in the final four in the BBC Food and Farming Awards 2006 (incredible considering we are both from relatively close areas in the country), in the Best Food Producer category, which I went on to win. Nichola is a valuable source of information on any food-related matter and her help and advice are very much appreciated. The following two recipes are reproduced with her kind permission.

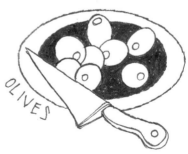

Arbroath Smokies in Parsley Sauce

You can either leave the Arbroath Smokies whole and serve the sauce separately or remove the fish from the skin and stir it into the sauce before serving. You can also use half fish stock and half milk if you prefer. Either way, it is simple but delicious.

Serves: 2
Preparation Time: 5 minutes
Cooking Time: 10 minutes

Ingredients
1 pair Arbroath Smokies
30g butter
30g plain flour
300ml milk or stock
salt and pepper to taste
30g (big handful) fresh parsley
15g butter (optional)

Set the Arbroath Smokies to warm in the oven. Whether whole or with the skin removed, I usually add a sprinkling of water and cover them so they don't dry out.

Melt the butter in a small saucepan and, when sizzling, stir in the flour. Allow to cook for a few minutes and then add the milk or stock, bit by bit, beating out any lumps in the early stages. When it is nice and smooth, boil rapidly for 3 minutes. It should coat the back of the spoon. If too thin, cook gently till thickened up a bit more and, if too thick, add a little more liquid. Season to taste.

While the sauce cooks, chop the parsley, not too fine. Stir into the sauce when ready to serve. If using the extra butter, beat this in just before serving. If taking the fish out of the skin, add the fish at this stage. Otherwise serve the sauce with the whole fish.

Arbroath Smokies and Nichola Fletcher's Green Leek Sauce

'This is the way I serve leeks nowadays – my way of not wasting anything. But with its gentle leek flavour and dramatic green colour, this both tastes and looks fantastic with the pure white flesh of Arbroath Smokies.' (Nichola Fletcher)

Serves: 4
Preparation Time: 10 minutes
Cooking Time: 20 minutes

Ingredients
2 pairs Arbroath Smokies
4–6 medium leeks
600ml water
60g butter
60g plain flour
salt and pepper to taste

Set the Arbroath Smokies to warm in the oven. Whether whole or with the skin removed, I usually add a sprinkling of water and cover them so they don't dry out.

Remove the roots and the outer layer of the leeks if dirty and slice off the very top of the green part and any really leathery pieces. Wash all the green parts thoroughly to remove any grit and chop into about 2cm lengths. Cover with the water and simmer till cooked (about 10

WATER

Butter.

PLAIN

FLOUR

LEEKS

minutes). Then blitz in a blender or with a food processor till it is a purée.

Cut the white part of the leeks into short pieces and simmer until cooked, then drain well.

While the white leeks cook, melt the butter in a small saucepan and, when sizzling, stir in the flour. Allow to cook for a few minutes and then add the green leek purée, bit by bit, beating out any lumps in the early stages. When it is nice and smooth, boil rapidly for 3 minutes. It should coat the back of the spoon. If too thin, cook gently till thickened up a bit more and, if too thick, add a little milk or water. Season to taste and pour it over the leeks and serve with the Arbroath Smokies.

Arbroath Smokie Patties with Mustard Dill Sauce

These patties can be made using leftover mashed potato from a previous meal. A delicious way to use up leftovers!

Serves: 6
Preparation Time: 45 minutes plus chilling time
Cooking Time: 10 minutes

Ingredients
For the patties:
1kg floury potatoes (Rooster or Maris Piper), peeled and
    halved if large
50g unsalted butter
2 leeks, white and green parts washed well and finely sliced
2 pairs Arbroath Smokies, boned and flaked
zest of 1 lemon
freshly ground black pepper
plain flour
2 tbsp olive oil

For the mustard dill sauce:
6 tbsp white wine
8 tbsp full-fat crème frâiche
3 tsp English mustard
1 tbsp fresh dill, chopped

6 eggs, to serve

DILL

Boil the potatoes for 20 minutes. Drain, season and mash with 25g of the butter.

Cook the leeks gently in the other 25g of butter.

Put the mashed potato in a large bowl and fold in the flaked Arbroath Smokies, leeks and lemon zest until well combined. Season with freshly ground black pepper. The mixture will make 12 patties; use flour to stop the mixture from sticking to your hands. Chill in the fridge – if they are not chilled, they will 'spread' when fried.

Heat the olive oil in a frying pan and cook the patties for a couple of minutes on each side until browned.

For the sauce, put all of the ingredients into a small pan and heat gently until piping hot.

Poach the eggs.

Serve the patties with a poached egg on top and then dress with the mustard dill sauce.

Arbroath Smokie and Seafood Pilau

This dish is based on a recipe by Angela Boggiano (Zesty Smoked Haddock and Prawn Pilau). Angela is a highly respected food writer and stylist and one third of Fork Ltd. She is the Food Director for *Delicious Magazine* and, over the years, has advised on several TV food programmes and written numerous food articles and recipes. This recipe is adapted with her kind permission. For added luxury, you can add a few mussels and/or queen scallops.

Serves: 4
Preparation Time: 15 minutes
Cooking Time: 30 minutes

Ingredients
2 tbsp olive oil
1 onion, finely chopped
1 clove of garlic, crushed
2cm piece fresh ginger, grated
350g basmati rice, rinsed and drained
1½ tsp ground cumin
1 tsp turmeric
grated zest and juice of 1 lime plus lime wedges to serve
700ml boiling water
1 pair Arbroath Smokies, boned and flaked
200g peeled, cooked cold water prawns
50g unsalted cashew nuts, toasted and split into halves
large bunch of fresh coriander, roughly chopped

LIME

CORIANDER

Heat the oil in a large frying pan, add the onion and cook gently until translucent. Add the garlic and ginger and cook for a further 2 minutes.

Add the rice, cumin, turmeric and lime zest and cook for 2 minutes, stirring to coat the rice with the spices. Pour in the boiling water and once it has returned to the boil reduce the heat, cover and simmer for 15 minutes or until the rice is tender and all the liquid has been absorbed.

Fold in the flaked Arbroath Smokies, prawns, lime juice, nuts and most of the coriander.

Garnish with the remaining coriander and serve immediately with lime wedges.

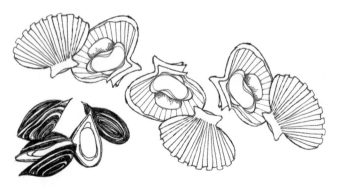

Arbroath Smokie Fish Cakes

This recipe is exactly the same as the one I use for the fishcakes that I make and sell for my weekly slot at the Fife Farmers' Markets. You can easily change it a little if you want by substituting some of the smokie meat for a little hot-smoked salmon or hot smoked trout, but I think it is best when made purely with smokies. Cooking them in the oven is the best way but they can just as easily be fried in a little oil if you wish.

Serves: 4
Preparation time: 50 minutes plus chilling time
Cooking Time: 20 minutes

Ingredients
450g peeled potatoes (floury varieties such as Rooster, Maris Piper or Desiree)
25g unsalted butter
1 tbsp crème fraîche
2 tbsp fresh flat leaf parsley, chopped
1 pair Arbroath Smokies, boned and flaked
50g Scottish mature Cheddar cheese, grated
1 large free-range egg, beaten
Ruskoline crumb dressing

Place the potatoes into a pan of cold salted water, bring to the boil and simmer for 20 minutes or until cooked. Drain thoroughly, and then mash together with the butter and crème fraîche. Stir in the chopped parsley and allow the mixture to cool.

Preheat the oven to 180°C/350°F/Gas 4.

Add the flaked Arbroath Smokies and cheese to the potato mixture and combine together using your hands, (you may want to use disposable vinyl gloves for this), making sure that everything is mixed evenly. The fishcakes now need to be shaped; this can be done roughly by simply moulding a cake shape with your hands but I find the best way is to use a pastry ring cutter of approximately 75mm wide x 25mm deep. Once shaped, dip each fishcake in the beaten egg mixture and coat with the Ruskoline crumb dressing. Place on a lightly oiled baking tray and cook for 20 minutes.

Kedgeree

Serves: 4
Preparation Time: 10 minutes
Cooking Time: 30 minutes

Ingredients
4 free-range eggs
1 tbsp olive oil
25g unsalted butter
1 onion, chopped
1 cinnamon stick
½ tsp ground turmeric
2 tsp mild curry powder
1 bay leaf
200g basmati rice, rinsed and drained
100ml whole milk
1 pair Arbroath Smokies, boned and flaked
300ml boiling water
freshly ground black pepper
2 tbsp fresh coriander, roughly chopped

Bring a pan of water to the boil, gently lower in the eggs
and cook for 5 minutes. Drain and cool in cold water.

Heat the oil and butter in a large pan. Fry the onion
for 5 minutes until translucent. Add the spices and bay
leaf and cook for a further 2 minutes.

Add the rice and stir to coat in the oil and spices.
Add the milk and water and bring to the boil. Cover,

reduce the heat and cook for 15 minutes without disturbing.

Remove the cinnamon stick and bay leaf and gently mix the flaked Arbroath Smokies in with the rice and season with black pepper.

Remove the shells from the hard-boiled eggs and cut into quarters.

Serve with the hard-boiled eggs and garnish with coriander.

Note: you may wish to add 125g of cooked peas when you fold in the Arbroath Smokies.

Arbroath Smokie and Roasted Vegetable Bake

Serves: 2
Preparation Time: 1 hour
Cooking Time: 15 minutes

Ingredients
3 peppers – 1 each of red, orange and yellow – deseeded and
    cut into 3cm chunks
6 shallots, peeled and halved
1 red onion, peeled and divided into 8 chunks
1 courgette, sliced
1 tbsp fresh oregano
freshly ground black pepper
olive oil
unsalted butter
1 pair Arbroath Smokies, boned and flaked
150g Mozzarella cheese, drained and cut into 2cm cubes
75g breadcrumbs

Heat the oven to 200°C/400°F/Gas 6.

Scatter the pepper chunks, shallot halves, onion
chunks and courgette slices onto baking sheets; you will
need two trays so that the vegetables don't overlap and to
allow them to cook properly. Scatter with the oregano,
season with black pepper and then drizzle with olive oil.
Toss the vegetables in the oil to coat and bake for 30–40
minutes, turning halfway through the cooking time.

Reduce the oven heat to 190°C/375°F/Gas 5.

Coat a baking dish generously with butter. Scatter the flaked Arbroath Smokies into the dish. Cover with the roasted vegetables. Dot the cubes of Mozzarella amongst the mixture. Scatter over the breadcrumbs (they may not cover it all but it does not matter) and bake in the oven for 15 minutes.

Serve with a fresh green salad.

Suppers and Snacks

BUTTER

Soured Cream

FLAKED SMOKIE

SCOTTISH MATURE CHEDDAR

CHIVES

Arbroath Smokie Jacket Potatoes with Sour Cream and Chives

_____

Serves: 2
Preparation Time: 10 minutes
Cooking Time: 1 hour 30 minutes

Ingredients
2 large baking potatoes
salt
2 large knobs of unsalted butter
1 Arbroath Smokie, boned and flaked
2 tbsp soured cream
2 tbsp fresh chives, chopped
freshly ground black pepper
100g Scottish mature Cheddar, grated

_____

Preheat the oven to 180°C/350°F/Gas 4.

Wash the potatoes and dry thoroughly. Prick the skin all over and rub with salt. Place the potatoes on a baking sheet and bake for 1 hour 20 minutes.

You can save some time here by microwaving the baking potatoes first. For two potatoes, after pricking, place on a plate and wrap in a wet piece of kitchen towel. Microwave on high (1000W) for 6 minutes, turn over and repeat. Remove the towel, rub with salt and place on a tray in the oven for 30–40 minutes. However, for me personally, I prefer my potatoes properly baked in the oven to get that lovely texture to the skins – it's worth waiting for!

Remove the potatoes, keeping the oven on. Cut the potatoes in half lengthways. Scoop out the potato from each half into a bowl and put the skins to one side.

Mix in the butter, flaked Arbroath Smokie, sour cream and chives with the potato and season with freshly ground pepper.

Fill the potato skins with the mixture, sprinkle over the cheese and return to the oven for 5 minutes until the cheese is golden and bubbling.

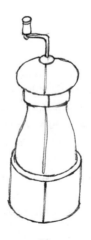

Arbroath Smokie, Leek and Sweet Potato Pasties

With the Cornish pasty and Arbroath Smokies both having the PGI status now, and my wife Su being a fiercely proud Cornish lass – or Jenny, as the Cornish say – I simply had to include a recipe here that combined both products. The following recipe is all purely her creation and I'm quite sure you'll like it. A real Cornish pasty's core ingredients are beef, potato, swede and onion so, rather than simply substituting the beef with fish, we've had to adapt things a bit and use different vegetables that complement the smokies but still retain something of the original pasty character. These little pasties make great picnic food.

Serves: 4
Preparation Time: 30 minutes
Cooking Time: 30 minutes

Ingredients
500g ready-made shortcrust pastry
1 pair Arbroath Smokies, boned and flaked
freshly ground black pepper
2 leeks, white and pale green parts, sliced
350g sweet potato, peeled and diced small
40g unsalted butter
milk or 1 free-range egg, beaten (optional)

Preheat the oven to 180°C/350°F/Gas 4.

Divide the pastry into quarters. Lightly flour the work surface and roll one quarter out into a circle approximately 25cm in diameter. Fold the pastry in half, place the rolling pin against the straight edge, and unfold, so that the rolling pin is supporting half of the pastry.

Place a quarter of the flaked Arbroath Smokies onto the pastry base, leaving a border of 2cm to seal later. Season with black pepper. Sprinkle a quarter of the sliced leeks, followed by a quarter of the diced sweet potato. Cube 10g of the butter and dot over the contents.

Wet the border of the pastry with water. Carefully stretch the top half over the top to meet the border and seal by crimping the edges together. Make a small hole in the top to let any steam escape. If desired, brush with milk or beaten egg and place on a baking sheet.

Repeat the process to make 4 pasties in total.

Cook for 40–45 minutes until golden brown. Can be eaten hot or cold.

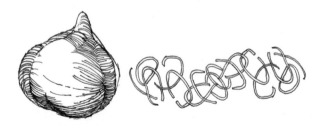

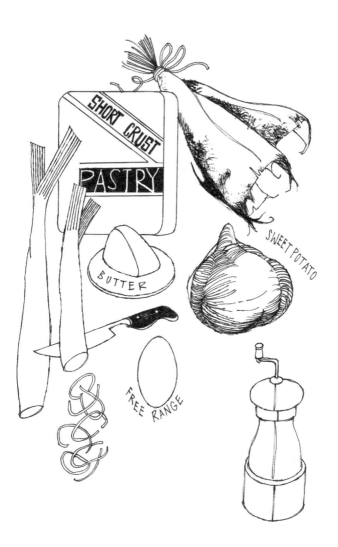

SHORT CRUST

PASTRY

BUTTER

SWEET POTATO

FREE RANGE

Arbroath Smokie and Spinach Gratin

Serves: 4
Preparation Time: 30 minutes
Cooking Time: 30 minutes

Ingredients
1 tbsp olive oil
25g unsalted butter
1 garlic clove, crushed or finely chopped
500g fresh spinach, washed
2 pairs Arbroath Smokies, boned and flaked
250ml crème fraîche (full- or half-fat)
2 large ripe tomatoes, thinly sliced
125g Gruyère cheese, grated
1 tbsp fresh coriander, chopped

Heat the oven to 180°C/350°F/Gas 4.

Melt the olive oil and butter in a large saucepan. Fry the garlic for a few minutes. Add the spinach and turn frequently until wilted. Drain well in a sieve or colander, otherwise the final dish will be very watery.

Cover the base of a large baking dish with the spinach.

Scatter the flaked Arbroath Smokies over the spinach and then dot with teaspoons of the crème fraîche. Cover with the sliced tomatoes, pressing them into the crème fraîche to ensure that the contents are fairly level.

Top with the Gruyère cheese and bake for 30

minutes. If required, finish under a hot grill for 2–3 minutes.

Garnish with the coriander and serve with fresh granary bread.

Arbroath Smokie Gratins

Serves: 4
Preparation Time: 15 minutes
Cooking Time: 25 minutes

Ingredients
1 pair Arbroath Smokies, boned and flaked
2 tbsp olive oil
1 onion, finely chopped
2 cloves garlic, crushed
1 red chilli, seeds discarded and very finely chopped
225g mushrooms, finely sliced
1 tbsp fresh oregano
freshly ground black pepper
50g Grana Padano cheese, grated

Preheat the oven to 200°C/400°F/Gas 6.

Bone and flake the Arbroath Smokies and reserve.

Heat the olive oil in a frying pan and add the onions, garlic and chilli. Fry gently until the onion is soft – do not allow to brown. Add the mushrooms and fry for 3 minutes.

Stir in the flaked Arbroath Smokies and oregano and season with black pepper.

Divide the mixture between four ramekins, pressing the mixture in firmly, and then top with the Grana Padano cheese.

Cook in the oven for 15 minutes.

Tagliatelle with Creamy Lemon Smokie

This recipe is kindly reproduced with permission from Jan Rees of Ellon. With it, she won the BBC Good Food Pasta Recipe of the Year Award in 1998.

Serves: 2
Preparation time: 10 minutes
Cooking Time: 12 minutes

Ingredients
150g tagliatelle
1 Arbroath Smokie
150ml crème fraîche
finely grated rind of 1 unwaxed lemon
small handful of finely chopped parsley

Bring a large pan of water to the boil, add the tagliatelle and cook until 'al dente'.

Meanwhile, bone and flake the Arbroath Smokie, keeping the flakes as big as possible.

Warm the crème fraîche in a pan. Add the lemon zest, parsley and fish, stirring gently to avoid breaking up the flakes.

Drain the tagliatelle, divide between 2 warmed bowls and spoon the sauce over.

Garnish with extra lemon rind and parsley if you wish.

Arbroath Smokie Omelette

This recipe is based on James Martin's take on Omelette Arnold Bennett which he used in the TV series *Castle in the Country*. The programme followed on from a day's filming where James worked with me for a whole morning on my stall at the Kirkcaldy Farmers' Market. James was genuinely very enthusiastic and hands-on and got involved in absolutely everything, even boning and serving smokies directly to my customers – much to their delight! I think he will always remember the day well. We had just got everything set up and the fires lit in the smokie barrels when the wind changed round 180 degrees. This meant that the smoke blew back through the stall most of the morning making it a pretty full-on smokie experience for him and the film crew!

Serves: 2
Preparation Time: 10 minutes
Cooking Time: 10 minutes

Ingredients
6 free-range eggs
freshly ground black pepper
25g unsalted butter
1 Arbroath Smokie, boned and flaked
50ml double cream
50g Parmesan cheese, grated
1 tbsp fresh herb – coriander, chives or parsley – chopped

The recipe is enough for two people but I prefer to halve the ingredients and make two separate omelettes.

Preheat the grill to high.

Whisk the eggs together with the black pepper.

Melt the butter in a non-stick frying pan (ideally with a heatproof handle) and swirl it around to coat the base of the pan.

Pour in the eggs and, as they start to set, drag the edges of the omelette back, allowing the uncooked egg to run underneath folds of cooked egg.

When the omelette is set underneath, scatter over the flaked Arbroath Smokie.

Pour the cream over the top, sprinkle with Parmesan cheese and place under a hot grill until cooked.

Slide it on to a warmed plate, garnish with fresh herbs of your choice and serve.

Arbroath Smokie with Broccoli and Cream

This recipe is based on one of Nigel Slater's recipes which I have adapted for Arbroath Smokies. I think Nigel would approve since, as part of the judging process for BBC Food Producer of the Year Award 2006, I took him to Auchmithie, the true home of the Arbroath Smokie. He was treated to a fish fresh off the barrel, which he described as 'eye-opening, a revelation in taste and texture'.

Serves: 2
Preparation Time: 15 minutes
Cooking Time: 30 minutes

Ingredients
250g broccoli, divided into small florets
unsalted butter
1 pair Arbroath Smokies, boned and flaked
freshly ground black pepper
30ml double cream
4 tbsp fresh breadcrumbs

Heat the oven to 200°C/400°F/Gas 6.

Cook the broccoli in plain boiling water or microwave for 4 minutes on full power (1000W). Drain well.

Coat a baking dish generously with butter. Scatter the flaked Arbroath Smokies and broccoli into the baking dish. Season with plenty of black pepper, pour over the cream and scatter over the breadcrumbs.

Bake for 20–25 minutes.

BROCCOLI

DOUBLE Cream

BUTTER

Arbroath Smokie and Spinach Tortilla

Another of my wife Su's creations. She spends a lot of time visiting her parents in Spain. Tortillas are a popular speciality found all over Spain. There are many variations but they typically include eggs, potato and onions. Other ingredients, such as tuna, red peppers and chorizo, are often added but we saw the opportunity to include Arbroath Smokies!

Serves: 2
Preparation Time: 15 minutes
Cooking Time: 20 minutes

Ingredients
15g unsalted butter
1 tbsp olive oil
1 small onion, sliced
2 medium potatoes, peeled and finely diced
1 pair Arbroath Smokies, boned and flaked
150g spinach
4 large free-range eggs
50ml double cream
½ tsp freshly grated nutmeg
freshly ground black pepper
1½ tbsp freshly chopped chives
50g Scottish mature Cheddar cheese, grated
100g baby leaf salad

Heat butter and oil in a large frying pan (ideally with a heatproof handle) and fry the onion and potato for 10 minutes, until the potato is starting to brown.

Add the spinach, stir in and wilt for 2 minutes.

Add the flaked Arbroath Smokies.

In a jug or bowl, beat together eggs, cream and nutmeg. Season well with black pepper and add 1 tablespoon of chives. Pour the creamy mixture into the pan evenly so that it covers the potato and fish. Cook for a few minutes until the egg mixture is set underneath.

Meanwhile, preheat the grill to high.

Sprinkle the cheese over the dish and place under the grill for 3–5 minutes, taking care to keep the handle away from the heat. When the egg is cooked through and the cheese is bubbling, remove and sprinkle with remaining chives.

Serve with baby leaf salad.

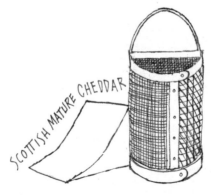

Foodie thoughts from
a Sassenach's kitchen

Stephen Hill is a customer of mine who has become a very good friend. He is a real foodie through and through and here are some of his interesting and alternative ideas on Arbroath Smokies and complementary flavours.

In this modern world, we now have the means and ability to transport local specialist foods quickly over long distances, thus enabling foodies like myself to experience such delicacies in tip-top condition. So, our smokies have arrived by overnight courier and are sitting in the fridge – what the heck do we do with them now?!

Remember, smokies are a salted, fully cooked and – well – very smoky-flavoured fish. So combining them with most subtle or sweet flavours isn't really going to work. Think tart or sour tastes. And because smokies are already fully cooked, they work just as well in cold dishes such as salads and pâtés as in hot repasts.

Here are a few PRESENTATIONAL ideas which, as it happens, work equally well hot or cold.

Smokie meat on a bed of lightly baked pink rhubarb with mixed green and micro leaves plus, perhaps, just a couple of baby new potatoes. Bake the rhubarb in the normal way mixing no more than a couple of lavender essence drops (be careful, lavender can easily overpower a dish!) to the baking liquor. Don't over-bake the rhubarb – try to retain the stalk shape – and don't use green-stemmed rhubarb – it's not good eye-candy and I think its tartness will overpower the smokie. Lightly dress the leaves with a simple vinaigrette. Personally, I would omit any other salad items – tomatoes, cucumber, spring onions, radishes, etc. – on the basis that less is more. Alternatively, replace the rhubarb with poached, well-drained damsons or with a sieved, gloopy sauce made from gooseberries in white wine with elderflower cordial and a little lime juice.

Follow a mackerel pâté recipe using smokie meat instead. Again, don't add 'unnecessary' ingredients or flavours – OK, cream and butter are good!

For a really quick snack, put a cold, grilled or microwaved smokie on a dinner plate with wholemeal bread and butter, slices from a tart apple (e.g. Granny Smiths) and a good, old-fashioned chutney – rhubarb, strawberry, cranberry and fig. The acidity of the vinegar in the chutney brings just that necessary tart 'edge' to the plate. But you do need to experiment as some chutneys and pickles will not work.

Above all – enjoy 'The Smokie Experience'!

Stephen Gwillam Hill

Where can I buy genuine Arbroath Smokies?

At the time of writing (2013), none of the major super-market chains currently stocks genuine Arbroath Smokies although this may change in the future. Your local fishmonger should be your first port of call although many delicatessens and farm shops now stock them too. Wherever you buy from, always look out for the PGI logo – this is the mark of authenticity that gives you the guarantee that you are buying the real thing. You can of course order them directly from me in Arbroath via mail order through my website – www.arbroathsmokies.net.

The website has an easy-to-order facility allowing you to buy Arbroath Smokies and other smoked fish speciali-ties online, which I normally despatch twice a week via 24-hour courier. You could also take a trip to Arbroath and visit one of the many smokehouses dotted around the 'Fit o' the Toon', many of whom smoke fish every day. Please feel free to contact me at iain@arbroathsmokies.net for more information regarding your visit as there are several 'Spink' fish businesses in Arbroath and I am not related to any of them!

Alternatively, have a look at the 'Events Calendar' on my website and find out where I will be doing my Arbroath Smokie-making demonstrations. Come along and get one from me fresh, hot and juicy, straight from the barrel, and experience a truly mouth-watering piece of Scotland's fishing heritage at its very, very best.

Finally, if I have made any mistakes with any of the recipes or perhaps you want to suggest your own little tweaks to them or even have a recipe of your own that you would like to share, then please drop me an email as I would love to hear from you.

Contacts:
Email – iain@arbroathsmokies.net
Internet – www.arbroathsmokies.com
and www.arbroathsmokies.net
Facebook –
www.facebook.com/IainRSpinkArbroathSmokies
Twitter – @IainRSpink